Economically Developing Countries

Ghana

Steve Brace
ACTIONAID Education Officer

This book has been produced in association with ACTIONAID. ACTIONAID works with some of the poorest children, families and communities in 20 countries in Africa, Asia and Latin America. Through both long-term development programmes and emergency relief, it aims to help people secure lasting improvements in their quality of life. ACTIONAID (charity no.274467) has received Wayland's fixed authorship fee for contributing the text to this publication.

Wayland

Economically Developing Countries

Bangladesh   India
Brazil   Mexico
China   Nigeria
Egypt   Peru
Ghana   The Philippines

Cover and contents page: Farmers sell their produce at a small market.
Title page: A family compound at a Ghanaian village near Lake Volta.

Picture acknowledgements
ACTIONAID 29, 30 (bottom), 31, 33, 35, 36, 37, 42; Bruce Coleman/Hans Reinhard
10; Mary Evans 20; Eye Ubiquitous 21, 39 (Thelma Sanders); Hutchison 13
(A. Tully), 14 (Timothy Beddow), 23, 25 (A. Tully), 26 & 32 (Crispin Hughes), 43;
Impact/Caroline Penn cover, 3, 5, 7, 15, 17 (top), 19, 22, 28; Panos 1 (Betty Press), 6
(Bruce Paton), 12 (Betty Press), 16 (Gary John Norman), 24 (Betty Press), 27 (Liba
Taylor), 40 (Bruce Paton), 45 (Betty Press); Popperfoto 4; Tropix 8 (M & V Birley),
9 (D. Parker), 17 (bottom, M & V Birley), 18 (D Parker), 30 (top, M & V Birley), 34
(L. Brydon), 44 (M & V Birley). Maps and artwork by Peter Bull.

Series editor: Paul Mason
Editor: Marcella Forster
Series designer: Malcolm Walker

First published in 1994 by
Wayland (Publishers) Ltd
61 Western Road, Hove
East Sussex, BN3 1JD, England

© Copyright 1994 by Wayland (Publishers) Ltd

British Library Cataloguing in Publication Data
Brace, Steve
  Ghana. - (Economically Developing
  Countries series)
  I. Title II. Series
  330.9667

ISBN 0-7502-1002-8

Typeset by Kudos Design

Contents

Introduction

Ghana was the first sub-Saharan African nation to gain its independence from Britain. This new country was formed by combining the Gold Coast and the British Trust territory of Togoland.

On 6 March 1957, in the presence of the Duchess of Kent, Ghana's independence ceremony took place. Britain's flag, the Union Jack, was lowered, and Ghana's red, green, gold and black flag was raised. With this, political power passed from the British to Kwame Nkrumah, who became Ghana's first African prime minister. He had previously been imprisoned by the British because of his demands for Ghanaian self-government. Nkrumah's rise to power was met with great optimism by Ghanaians, who would now be running their own affairs.

Since the 1950s Ghana has made great strides in improving the quality of life of its people. New hospitals, factories, power stations, schools, roads and towns have been built. Today, as a result of these improvements, Ghana is one of the most developed countries in Africa.

However, despite Ghana's many achievements, it remains a poor nation compared with developed countries such as Britain, Australia and the USA. There are rich and poor people in Ghana, as in any country, but many Ghanaians live in absolute poverty. This means they have poor access to basic facilities, such as clean water, health care and education. An important task facing

Dr Kwame Nkrumah was Ghana's first African prime minister.

Millions of poor people in Ghana do not have access to safe drinking water. This well in Nsawkaw, Brong Ahafo Region, has improved people's lives considerably by providing water that is free from disease.

Ghana is involving these very poor people in development.

Ghana receives outside help for development. In 1991 it was given $724 million official development assistance by rich countries and international organizations. International development charities, such as ACTIONAID and Oxfam, are also working in Ghana.

Ghana is a country of marked contrasts, ranging from thriving business centres to slums and from prosperous cocoa farms to poor millet-growing fields, but throughout Ghana people know what they need to secure a successful future for themselves and for their children.

'We need more seeds, more varieties of seed, and we must have bullocks and ploughs to make our farming more productive.'
– Fatima Amando, Sapeliga, Upper East Region

The natural environment

Ghana is located in West Africa between the equator and the Tropic of Cancer. It covers 238,500 square kilometres – about the same area as Britain and less than a thirtieth the area of Australia. Ghana is bordered by three countries: Togo to the east, Burkina Faso to the north and the Ivory Coast to the west. Ghana's southern border forms 539 kilometres of coastline along the Gulf of Guinea.

LANDSCAPE

From the gently rolling coastal plain to the northern savannah, Ghana's landscape is generally flat and low lying. The main areas of upland are in the southeast, where the Akwapim Range reaches a height of over 800 metres. Ghana's highest point is Mount Afadjato at 885 metres.

Lake Bosumtwi is Ghana's only large natural lake. Lake Volta, in the east, is a huge artificial lake, covering 9,500 square kilometres. It was created when the River Volta was blocked by the Akosombo Dam, 110 kilometres inland. The River Volta drains 70 per cent of Ghana's land. Many of Ghana's rivers are seasonal. Some evaporate completely during the dry season.

Along Ghana's coast, there are many marshes, mangrove swamps, inlets and lagoons, such as Keta Lagoon in the east.

CLIMATE

Ghana has a tropical climate with three broad climatic zones: a hot and dry coast, a hot and wet interior, and a hot and dry north.

These women in Adaboya are among the 55 per cent of Ghana's population that rely on the land for their livelihood.

These women on the outskirts of Bolgatanga, in the dry Upper East Region, are carrying fuelwood, Ghana's most common source of energy. Electricity is usually available only in the towns and cities.

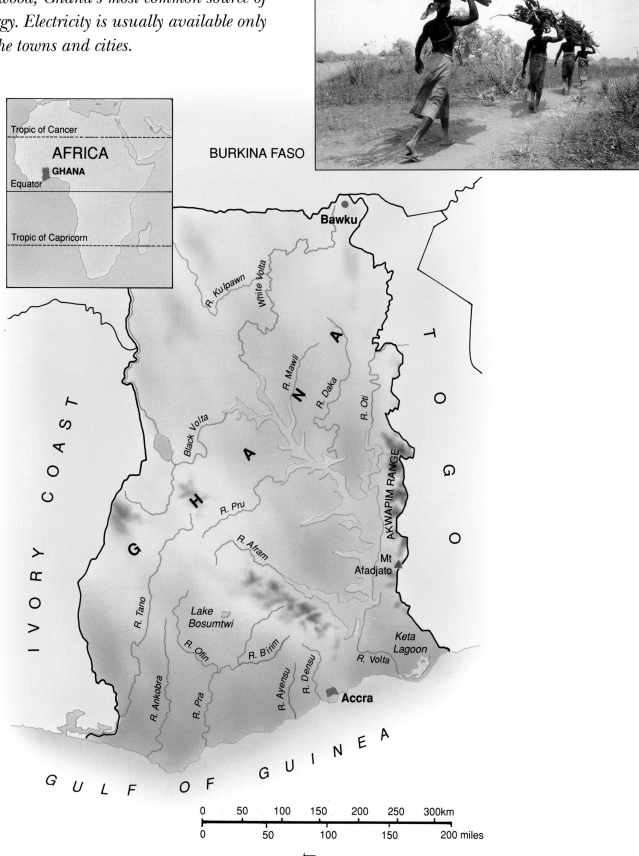

Tropic of Cancer

AFRICA
GHANA

Equator

Tropic of Capricorn

BURKINA FASO

Bawku

R. Kulpawn

White Volta

R. Mawli

R. Daka

R. Oti

G H A N A

Black Volta

R. Pru

R. Afram

AKWAPIM RANGE

Mt Afadjato

R. Tano

Lake Bosumtwi

Keta Lagoon

R. Ofin

R. Birim

R. Densu

R. Volta

R. Ankobra

R. Pra

R. Ayensu

Accra

I V O R Y   C O A S T

T O G O

G U L F   O F   G U I N E A

| 0 | 50 | 100 | 150 | 200 | 250 | 300km |

| 0 | 50 | 100 | 150 | 200 miles |

7

The red dust on these plants came from the Sahel Desert. It was deposited by the harmattan, a wind that blows across the north of Ghana in January and February.

Temperatures are highest in the months of March and April, when they reach over 30°C in northern regions. For most of the country there are two rainy seasons; the first is from April to June, and the second from September to November. Northern Ghana has only one rainy season, from June to September.

HARMATTAN

During January and February, a wind called *harmattan* blows across Ghana from the north and northeast, bringing hot and dry weather to the north. The air is hot because it has travelled over the arid Sahel Desert that lies to the north of Ghana. As the wind blows, it deposits a characteristic red dust, which it has picked up from the desert.

VEGETATION

Ghana's three broad climatic zones directly influence the country's vegetation. On the dry, narrow coastal strip the vegetation is coastal

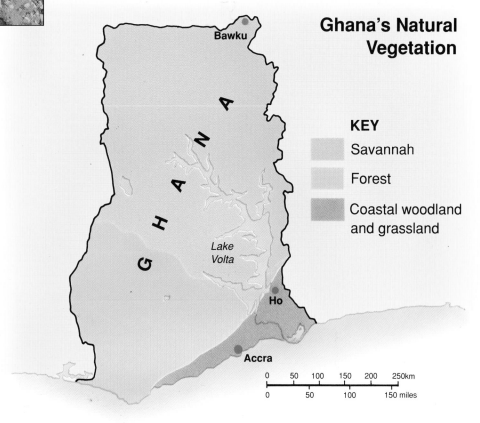

Ghana's Natural Vegetation

KEY

Savannah

Forest

Coastal woodland and grassland

Bawku

Lake Volta

Ho

Accra

| 0 | 50 | 100 | 150 | 200 | 250km |

| 0 | 50 | 100 | 150 miles |

This map shows Ghana's vegetation.

This Western Region tropical rainforest is part of a national park protected from over-exploitation.

Ghana's forests are an extremely important natural resource. They span over a third of the country, reaching from the southwest, along Ghana's border with the Ivory Coast, to Lake Volta in the east. These forests contain over 800 different types of tree, including mahogany and *wawa*.

savannah, characterized by scrub and tall grasses. Further north, where there is more rain, this vegetation changes to forest. In areas of very high rainfall there is evergreen rainforest. Where rainfall is lower, semideciduous trees – trees that shed their leaves and can survive periods of little rain – are more common. In the hot and dry north the main type of vegetation is savannah – plains of tall grasses. There are also scattered trees that can survive in the hostile hot, dry conditions, such as acacia.

RAINFALL AND TEMPERATURE

	Accra (coastal savannah)		**Ho** (forest zone/coastal woodland)		**Bawku** (interior savannah)	
	rainfall (mm)	temp (^{o}C)	rainfall (mm)	temp (^{o}C)	rainfall (mm)	temp (^{o}C)
Jan	18	27	36	28	0	27
Feb	38	28	79	29	5	29
Mar	56	28	140	28	13	31
Apr	76	28	145	28	48	32
May	127	27	178	27	99	29
Jun	191	26	183	26	117	27
Jul	51	24	109	25	168	27
Aug	15	24	84	25	241	26
Sep	38	25	150	26	201	26
Oct	58	26	191	26	56	28
Nov	36	27	79	27	8	27
Dec	25	27	51	27	5	27

WILDLIFE

Ghana's different environments, ranging from forest to savannah, support a wide range of wildlife. As well as over 720 species of bird, there are 222 species of mammal, including elephants, chimpanzees, antelopes and leopards. In an attempt to protect its wildlife, Ghana has designated over 10,000 square kilometres as national park, reserves or sanctuaries. In these areas the hunting of wildlife is illegal.

The human environment

Ghana's population of 14 million live in contrasting conditions. Thirty-two per cent live in towns and cities. The remaining 68 per cent live in rural areas. The south is most densely populated. Here, population density reaches 400 people per square kilometre, compared with 17 people per square kilometre in the north.

Most of Ghana's people are young: 64 per cent are under 25. Developed countries, like the USA and Britain, usually

POPULATION	
Accra	1,200,000
Kumasi	800,000
Sekondi-Takoradi	300,000
Tamale	200,000
Cape Coast	100,000
Ho	60,000
Bolgatanga	50,000

KEY

——— Main road

+++++++ Railway

------- Regional Boundary

✗ Airport

Ghana's Human Features

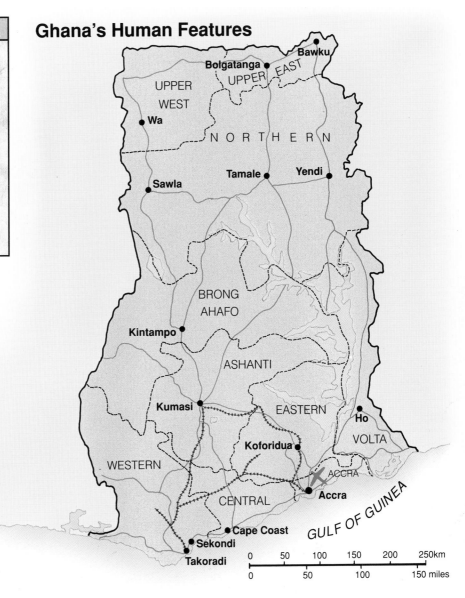

These women have established a fish-smoking business in Accra, Ghana's capital city. Smoking the fish preserves them so they can be sold throughout Ghana.

ECONOMIC ACTIVITY

Farming, fishing and forestry:
    59 per cent
Services, office work, retail:
    30 per cent
Manufacturing, carpentry:
    11 per cent
(Source: *Human Development Report*, 1993)

have a large proportion of old people and fewer young people. As young Ghanaians usually have children, Ghana is likely to see a large growth in population in the near future. At present the population is increasing by 3.2 per cent a year.

Ghana is predominantly a Christian country, but there are also Moslems and animists. Animism is Ghana's traditional religion. It involves ancestor worship and giving spiritual importance to natural events and features, such as the baobab tree, which is sometimes used as a shrine.

The official language of Ghana is English, an inheritance from British colonial rule. It is common for Ghanaians to speak at least two languages, and often many more. There are over seventeen main Ghanaian language groups.

RELIGION

Christians:
    55 per cent
Animists:
    32 per cent
Moslems:
    13 per cent

URBAN LIFE

Most of Ghana's major towns and cities are located in the south. The capital city is Accra, which has a population of 1.2 million. Other urban areas are Kumasi, Ho, Cape Coast, Sekondi and Takoradi, all of which are also in the south. There are fewer urban areas in the north of the country, the main ones being Tamale, Yendi, Bolgatanga, Wa and Bawku.

12

Urban centres contain a wide range of people. While there are many very poor people in Accra, you can walk down the city's exclusive Nkrumah Avenue and watch the rich spending a fortune.

Towns and cities are the main sites for industrial development. The Golden Triangle – covering Ashanti, and the Accra, Eastern and Central Regions – contains 60 per cent of Ghana's industries.

The growth of import substitution industries has been particularly important in Ghana. These industries were set up to manufacture goods that Ghana used to import – often at high prices – from developed countries. They provide new job opportunities and also reduce the amount of money Ghana has to spend buying products from abroad. Goods made by import substitution industries include

Accra is a city of contrasts. While there are many poor people, there are also people who are wealthy enough to shop at this Western-style supermarket.

textiles, paper, plastic goods, vehicles, footwear, pharmaceuticals, food and drink.

Ghana has also developed some modern industries. A new telecommunications project, supported by Japanese investment, aims to link Accra with the north of the country.

Below *Markets like this one are where town and countryside meet.*

RURAL LIFE

The most productive area of farming is in central Ghana, where fertile soil and a favourable climate encourage good crop yields. In the north low, irregular rainfall leads to poor yields.

Farming is usually performed in family groups, although wealthy farmers may hire labour. Both men and women work on the land. Women are also responsible for child care, looking after the home and time-consuming tasks such as collecting water and fuelwood.

Farm animals, such as goats, sheep and poultry, are kept throughout Ghana. Only relatively rich farmers can afford

Right *In rural areas people often use locally available materials to build their homes. This woman is plastering a wooden-framed home with mud.*

14

15

CROP TYPES

Ghana has two main types of crop: cash crops and food crops. Cash crops, such as cocoa, tobacco, rubber, coffee and pineapple, are grown to be sold, often overseas. Food crops, such as cassava, millet, yams, rice, sorghum and maize, are grown to be eaten.

This farmer will sell his oranges at a local market, then use the money to buy household goods.

to keep a small herd of cattle or a pair of bullocks for ploughing. Cattle can only be kept on the plains around Accra and in the north because these are the only areas free from the tsetse fly, which causes sleeping sickness in cattle.

Agricultural produce is an important source of income for individual families and also for Ghana as a whole. Thriving markets are widespread. Women play a very important role in these markets. The Ashanti women traders in particular are renowned for their business skills. Also, Ghana earns foreign currency from the sale of agricultural produce overseas. This is then used to buy goods from abroad that Ghana cannot provide for itself.

SHIFTING CULTIVATION

Many Ghanaian farmers use the shifting cultivation system of farming. A farmer clears a plot of land in the forest or on the savannah and burns the cut vegetation. The ash from the fire provides fertilizer for the soil. The land is used for a few years and then, when its fertility lessens, it is abandoned. The farmer then clears a new plot, leaving the old one to return to its natural vegetation and to regenerate its fertility. However, shifting cultivation is gradually being replaced by a more settled form of agriculture, with plots of land being permanently cultivated. This is because, with Ghana's growth in population and more people moving into the forest area to live, there is less land to farm.

Fishing is a major form of employment. These people live in Accra and fish in the Gulf of Guinea.

Many nonagricultural activities take place in rural areas. Forestry is particularly important, with over 70,000 people employed in the logging industry. Along Ghana's rivers, coastline and lakes, many people earn their living by fishing. The fish are often smoked for preservation and then sold.

MINERALS AND MINING

Ghana has many mineral resources, including gold, diamonds, bauxite and manganese. It is one of the world's largest suppliers of manganese. In 1993 there was a gold rush in Sapeliga in the Upper East Region. Many young men left their farms and animals in search of fortune. Wahabu Abubilla once worked as a cattle driver: 'The first time I found gold, I sold it for 28,000 cedis.' As a cattle driver it would have taken him six weeks to earn that much.

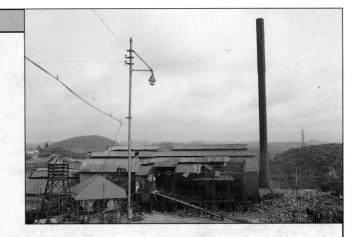

The Prestea gold mine. Gold is one of Ghana's most valuable mineral resources. In the north it is still mined by hand.

17

Constraints on Ghana's development

While northern Ghana suffers from low, irregular rainfall, other areas experience heavy downpours. These street sellers in the Eastern Region have been caught out in a tropical storm.

Ghana is well provided for, with a good range of human and natural resources. It has used its natural assets to achieve improvements in the quality of life for many of its people. Ghana has enormous potential for future development. However, in some areas, particularly outside towns and cocoa-growing areas, there is widespread poverty. There are several reasons for this.

ENVIRONMENTAL REASONS

Much of Ghana has rich environmental resources. However, other parts of the country do not. Northern Ghana has coarse, infertile soil and only one rainy season. The majority of farmers here cannot afford irrigation and so have only one harvest a year. The yield from this has to feed their families for twelve months.

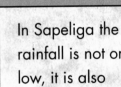

IRREGULAR RAINFALL

In Sapeliga the rainfall is not only low, it is also irregular. You can walk past two fields of millet, and one will be shoulder high, ready to harvest, while the other is only ankle high. This difference is caused by the rain suddenly stopping before the second field was planted.

These logs are destined for a sawmill at Kumasi.

Ghana's forests cover 8.2 million hectares – 34 per cent of the land. However, between 1981 and 1985 over 22,000 hectares of forest were cut down each year. The loss of forests can lead to erosion. Loose soil, once held in place by trees, is washed away by rain or blown away by wind, and the land's fertility is reduced. Poorer soil leads to lower crop yields, which means increased poverty. In addition, shifting cultivation farmers – who use fire to clear the forest – sometimes destroy seeds in the soil, preventing regrowth of the forest and reducing the land's fertility.

'*[Deforestation] is associated with population growth and economic development, and is directly linked to clearance for shifting cultivation and settled agriculture (principally cocoa), fuelwood and settlement.*' **– British Overseas Development Administration**

HISTORICAL REASONS

Before Ghana became independent, it was called the Gold Coast. This name demonstrates that European colonists viewed the country as a source of wealth.

Colonization has had a huge effect on Ghana's development. In the middle of the fifteenth century, Portuguese traders arrived in West Africa, including what is now Ghana. The Portuguese were later followed by the Spanish, Dutch and British. They came to trade. In particular they wanted gold dust, hence Ghana's old name. To protect their trade operations, the Europeans built a series of coastal forts. At one time there were 76 forts along the southern coast.

By the middle of the seventeenth century, Europe's interest had switched to slavery in order to provide free labour for plantations in the West Indies and America. Slavery had existed on the Gold Coast before, with slave raids into West Africa from the north. However, it increased dramatically under the Europeans. By the middle of the eighteenth century, over 100,000 slaves were being taken forcibly from this part of Africa every year. This created widespread disruption to local societies. The slave traders wanted only healthy, fit people. They took the

These Ashanti are being hunted for slavery by employees of the British colonists.

most productive individuals, leaving behind the old and weak, and they turned local tribes against each other by bribing them to raid slaves from each other.

Slavery was officially abolished in all British territories in 1823 because of pressure from Britain's Anti-Slavery Association – and because slave revolts in the West Indies were making slavery unprofitable. However, colonial interest in West Africa continued. In 1874, following military conflict and pacts with local leaders, the Gold Coast was proclaimed a British colony.

Britain's main interest was in resources that could be taken home. New crops, such as cocoa, were introduced. Transport links to the productive agricultural areas were established so that exportation would be easy.

Events did not always go smoothly for the British, however. There were many violent clashes with the Ashanti, who resisted British rule until their capital city, Kumasi, was totally destroyed by the British in 1874.

European colonists built forts, like this one at St. Jago, along Ghana's coast to protect their trade. First gold, then slaves were exported via these forts.

21

This is Ghana's only manganese mine, located in Nsuta Wassaw, Western Region. Ghana is one of the world's main exporters of manganese; in 1989 it produced 273,933 tonnes of this mineral.

Today, Ghana is still heavily reliant on the cocoa crop introduced by the British. The beans are exported from Ghana to developed countries, such as Britain, the USA, Germany and Holland, where they are used to make chocolate.

SOCIO-ECONOMIC REASONS

Ghana has a foreign debt of $3.1 million. It has to use 49 per cent of the money it earns from exports to pay off this debt. This is money that could be invested elsewhere in the economy. The roots of this situation are complex.

Ghana exports only a small range of unrefined goods, such as cocoa and minerals. By exporting so few products, Ghana is left very vulnerable to changes in their international price. Cocoa is Ghana's main source of income. At independence in 1957, it sold for £240 a tonne. By 1965 this had fallen to £100 a tonne. This drop in price led to a massive reduction in Ghana's income.

As well as coping with low international prices, Ghana's farmers have had to contend with the low prices offered to them by the Ghana Cocoa Marketing Board. This organization buys cocoa from the farmers and sells it overseas. During the 1970s and 1980s it offered farmers

This woman is collecting cocoa pods. Inside, there are valuable beans that can be sold overseas. However, the price of cocoa is not stable. When it falls, the income of the cocoa farmers - and of Ghana - drops drastically.

extremely low prices for their cocoa. As a result, many farmers stopped selling their harvest to the board, and *kalabule* (smuggling) increased. At one point, 50,000 tonnes of cocoa were being smuggled out of Ghana every year.

'Not only has our cocoa production fallen by almost one third but also the price our cocoa commands has fallen to one third of the price five years ago.' – **Jerry Rawlings, president of Ghana, 1983**

Kwame Nkrumah was Ghana's first democratically elected leader. Despite the very many positive changes he implemented in his country, by 1964 he had turned Ghana

23

into a one-party state. In 1966 he was overthrown in a military coup, setting the scene for a series of short-lived civilian and military governments. This instability brought allegations of corruption and repression. It seemed that Ghanaians risked punishment if they expressed views opposed to the policies of their government. In 1991 Amnesty International publicly criticized Ghana's human rights record. This is important because many countries are reluctant to give development funds to governments who repress their people.

A further problem is that Nkrumah used foreign investment to support development work. To get this investment, many concessions had to be made that were not in Ghana's best interests. For example, in 1965 a hydroelectric power station was built at the Akosombo Dam to provide electricity for homes and industry. The main industrial user was to be an aluminium smelting plant at Tema, owned by the US company Valco. This company secured a favourable deal, in which it received electricity at

The Akosombo Dam on the River Volta was built during Ghana's industrial development in the 1960s. The dam flooded 5 per cent of Ghana's land, much of which was valuable farmland.

very low prices. Nkrumah's aim had been for Valco to use Ghanaian bauxite in their plant, but instead the company imported supplies from the West Indies. Having spent vast amounts of money building the dam and flooding land in the hope that foreign firms like Valco would use Ghanaian resources, Ghana received few benefits.

STRUCTURAL ADJUSTMENT POLICIES (SAPs)

During the 1970s and the early 1980s, Ghana faced increasing economic problems. Income from cocoa was falling, debts were rising, and there were high rates of inflation (140 per cent) and unemployment. During this time, Flight Lieutenant Jerry Rawlings became Ghana's president. In an attempt to solve Ghana's economic problems, he led a drive against corruption and increased the prices paid to cocoa farmers.

In 1983 Rawlings sought loans from the International Monetary Fund (IMF), which lends money to countries with huge debts provided they change their economic policy.

Ghana received a very generous agreement on a loan of $500 million. It was used by the government to change the way the economy ran. The government reduced its involvement in economic decision-making and allowed businesses to operate more freely. Government-owned businesses were privatized and there were cuts in the number of government employees: in one year 28,000 people lost their jobs. Subsidies on household goods were removed, resulting in price rises of 30 per cent between 1983 and 1987.

These changes stabilized Ghana's economy. Inflation fell to less than 10 per cent, and economic growth of over 5 per cent was achieved. However, not everyone has benefited from these changes. Price rises have meant that people are spending less. This has reduced even further the income of women and of farmers in the north.

Flight Lieutenant Jerry Rawlings was elected president of Ghana in 1992.

'*The benefits of the structural adjustment programme have by-passed large sections of the productive population, especially farmers in northern Ghana and women in general.*'
– ACTIONAID report

Measuring development

*'How are we going to work to develop our community if there is nothing to eat before we go to work and there is nothing left when we get home?' – **Amado Assibi, farmer, Sapeliga, Upper East Region***

When we want to measure how developed a country is, we look at whether people can make choices in their lives that will lead them to a better future. The amount of money they earn is just a small part of this. While it is very important and affects their future opportunities, money does not cover every aspect of development.

These are some of the questions asked to discover how developed a country is:

- ❑ Do people have the opportunity to become educated?
- ❑ Do people have access to health services?
- ❑ Do people have access to safe water?
- ❑ Do people have a secure way of earning a living?
- ❑ To what age can people expect to live?
- ❑ What are the chances of babies dying before their fifth birthday?
- ❑ How much money do people have?

The answers to these questions give an indication of the quality of life experienced by a country's population. Most people in developed countries have a good quality of life. While people in Britain or the

This boy's stomach is swollen from malnourishment. He lives in a slum in Dixcove, Western Region. The open sewer that runs by his feet increases his risk of disease and creates an unpleasant environment.

'During the harvest there is food and the children turn up to school. But after Christmas our barns are empty. Parents cannot even afford a pencil, so many children stop coming. Only around August, when the early millet is harvested, do they return. Learning cannot be possible when there is no food.' – **Teacher, Sapeliga, Upper East Region**

LITERACY
Adults: 40 per cent

Education is vital for a developing country's future prosperity. As well as studying their own language, these pupils will learn English, an inheritance from colonial times.

USA may complain about the problems of modern living – for example, pollution or commuting – they do not suffer widespread malnutrition or illiteracy. These are problems common in developing countries, such as Ghana. Ghana is relatively prosperous compared with very poor African countries, like Mozambique, but is relatively poor when compared to the UK and the USA.

While statistics indicate quality of life at a national level, they do not show how people's daily lives are affected by level of development. They also do not show differences in development between parts of a country. For example, they do not show that in Ghana some areas have reaped great benefits from development while others have experienced few improvements.

An important aspect of development is sustainability: once changes have been made, can they be maintained year after year into the future? If not, no long-term

These men are constructing a well in Bolgatanga. Wells often fall into disrepair, and if the well is to provide long-term benefits, it is vital that the community is provided with the skills and resources to keep it working.

improvements will occur. Sustainability is not just dependent on careful use of resources such as farmland and forests. It also depends on whether or not people have the skills to protect their improvements. For example, will a poor community be able to put sufficient pressure on their local government officials to ensure their school is always supplied with teachers and resources? Educational opportunities for the future will only be preserved if they can do this.

COMPARISONS IN DEVELOPMENT

	Ghana	Mozambique	UK	Canada	USA
Percentage of children in primary education[1]	75	58	100	100	100
Number of people per nursing person[1]	1,670	4,280	240	140	160
Percentage of population with access to safe water[2]	56	22	*	*	*
Life expectancy in years[1]	55	47	75	77	76
Infant mortality rate per 1,000 births[1]	83	149	7	7	9
GNP per capita[1]	$400	$80	$16,550	$20,440	$22,240

[1] *World Bank Report, 1993* [2] *Human Development Report, 1993*
* No figures available, but most people in these countries have access to safe water

Development in the city

Accra is Ghana's bustling capital city, situated on the coast. It has all the characteristics you would associate with a city in a developed country: international airports, banks, shops, sports grounds, offices, cinemas – and traffic jams! However, there are also scenes more common in developing countries: street markets, newspaper sellers walking between lines of traffic, and slums.

Ringway Estate, Accra

Modern technology has provided one Accra family with the opportunity for economic development.

B K and Patience Sencherey live with their four children on the Ringway Estate in a prosperous area in eastern Accra. They have lived here for eight years. The area is well maintained and has electricity and water, as well as many local amenities, such as cinemas and shops.

The SYenchereys are an affluent family and illustrate how many Ghanaians have used their entrepreneurial skills to build up successful

The Sencherey family manage a successful restaurant and an office block. As a result, they enjoy a comfortable lifestyle and their children have the opportunity of a prosperous future.

Ghana's wealthy enjoy a comfortable life-style. Some can afford to live in houses like this one in Accra and may own cars and luxury goods, such as televisions and video recorders.

businesses. In fact, this family have a better life-style than some people in developed countries.

The family own a block of modern offices called Trinity House on Ring Road East in Accra. Their own business, Kwick Kall, is situated in this

'We have seen a lot of changes [on the Ringway Estate]. Many people have come to live here because it is rapidly becoming a commercial area. Many medium- and small-sized businesses are coming up [growing]. New restaurants, supermarkets, grocery stores, boutiques and offices are springing up fast in this area.'
– B K Sencherey, businessman, Accra

block. It offers secretarial and office services to the public. The Senchereys run their business together. Many Ghanaian women are involved in business as well as being

The Senchereys' Kwick Kall Business Centre in Accra provides secretarial and office services to the public.

responsible for looking after the home and children.

Inside Kwick Kall there are computer terminals and modern communications equipment that would not look out of place in an office in London, Sydney or New York. However, these facilities are relatively scarce in Ghana, where only six people in every thousand own a telephone. Most Ghanaians go to offices like Kwick Kall when they need to make a telephone call.

As well as owning Trinity House and running the Kwick Kall Centre, the Senchereys own a restaurant called Kookers, which serves Ghanaian and European food.

The Senchereys drive between home and work. Cars are a mark of prosperity in Ghana: less than 0.1 per cent of the population own one.

In common with most Ghanaians, Patience and B K Sencherey want their four children to do well at school. Josephine and Baffour attend primary school, while Kojo attends a

Mr Sencherey in the family restaurant, Kookers, which serves European and Ghanaian food.

*'[I want] to give our children a good education so they can be useful citizens for the future.' – **Patience Sencherey, businesswoman, Accra***

nursery and Nana goes to a creche.

The businesses the Sencherey family run provide wealth for themselves and have a beneficial effect on the Ghanaian economy. From the secretaries in the Kwick Kall Centre to the cooks in Kookers, people are employed and earning a wage. This means that the wealth the Senchereys generate is spread widely.

The Senchereys want to see their business flourish, not only so that they can increase their profits but also so they can employ more people and help other families. They also look forward to an improved national economy where life will become less difficult for the ordinary person.

Nima

Nima is one of Accra's many slum areas. Slums are usually located on wasteground, such as along railway tracks or on city outskirts. They are characterized by widespread poverty, a poor environment, poorly erected buildings and a lack of basic services, such as piped water, electricity and sanitation. In Accra, over 700,000 people do not have access to sanitation.

'Because accommodation in Accra is very difficult to come by, more and more people have moved here [to the slums] and the population has increased tremendously. Here accommodation is cheaper, but not very decent. Many essential facilities are still lacking.' – **Robert Anaman, butcher, Accra**

Slums often begin when people put up makeshift homes without permission. Over a number of years, what may have started as a few

Nima, one of Accra's slums, has few amenities. Open sewers are common, the houses are poorly built and few people have piped water.

Mohammed and Fatmatu Musa with their children. The couple are working hard to provide a good future for their children.

ramshackle buildings can develop into a permanent and established community.

Mohammed Musa, Fatmatu Musa and their five children have lived in such a community in Nima since 1965. Mohammed's main business is as a butcher. He is a middle man and buys meat from the slaughterhouses and then sells it to customers in Nima's local markets. Fatmatu is a petty trader, selling scarves and pans. Their eldest daughter, Aishatu, also contributes towards the family's welfare. She has just finished school. Aishatu is a trained dressmaker and earns money by sewing at home.

Some people living in Nima have jobs elsewhere in Accra, but most work in the local area. Typical jobs include petty trade (selling fruit, vegetables and household goods); small-scale manufacturing, such as carpentry; and service jobs, such as shoe repair and food preparation. However, there are also many people who do not have work.

Starting development work in slum areas can be difficult. These communities are made up of people who have few resources of their own

'The residents here are from mixed tribes and it is difficult to mobilize them for self-help development work. Also, we don't receive any assistance from other organizations or church groups.'
– Agnes Oparebea, Accra

This petty trader runs a haberdashery shop in Nima.

and who have migrated into an area where they know nobody. However, in Nima there are some positive signs of development. For example, Mohammed belongs to a business credit group, which helps its members with loans if they are in financial difficulty. This reduces the chance of people falling into debt with local money lenders, who charge extortionate rates of interest.

Despite their living conditions, people in the slums still want to secure the best possible opportunities for themselves and for their children. There are often no government schools in these areas. The nearest one to Nima is over four kilometres away. Even when schools are within reach, the fees can cause financial hardship. However, the Musas are managing to educate all their children.

Development in the countryside

'The farmers are the people feeding the masses.' – Offei Hanson, cocoa farmer, Asikasu-Odumase, Eastern Region

Agriculture is vital to Ghana's future prosperity because cash crops like cocoa and pineapples can earn valuable foreign currency. Some Ghanaian farmers are relatively wealthy and can take action to improve their lives, but others are poor and in need of development aid.

Asikasu-Odumase

Asikasu-Odumase is a village located in Ghana's forest zone in the Eastern Region. The nearest town is Koforidua, 60 kilometres north of Accra, so the village is close to Ghana's important urban areas. Asikasu-Odumase has good agricultural resources, with fertile soil and a high rainfall. Cocoa, a cash crop, dominates the local economy.

Opanyin Belle and Offei Hanson farm cocoa and other crops in Asikasu-Odumase. Both own large areas of farmland and so are relatively prosperous. Poorer farmers have to rent land for their farms. One of the

Offei Hanson selects some pineapples from his farm in Asikasu-Odumase, Eastern Region. The fertile soil and high rainfall in this area leads to good crop yields.

35

COCOA

Cocoa is grown on almost 40 per cent of Ghana's agricultural land and accounts for about 40 per cent of the country's export earnings. It was introduced to West Africa by European colonists, who brought it from South America during the nineteenth century. By 1915 Ghana was the world's largest cocoa producer, only being overtaken by the Ivory Coast and Brazil in the 1980s.

Cocoa trees take up to three years to mature before their pods can be harvested. Inside each pod are cocoa beans. The beans are dried then sold.

problems Offei faces is having to hire extra workers to farm all his land. Opanyin is planning to build two houses, one in Nsuata and a second in his home town of Kodiabe.

Dora Dede and Faustina Kwasibea, Offei Hanson's two wives, grow food crops for the family, including cassava, plantain, peppers and bananas. The produce is sold at the market in Anum-Apapam, about three kilometres away, and the proceeds are used to buy other goods. The Hanson family buy food;

others buy kerosene to fuel lamps, and household items such as pans and clothing.

The prosperity of these farmers is demonstrated by their investment in education and the work they have undertaken to improve their lives. Both families have put their children through primary and into secondary school, which is a major financial commitment. In Opanyin's case it meant paying school fees for eight children. He acknowledges that not everyone can afford such costs.

The local community has worked hard to make improvements. However, people here do see a role for external help, particularly in the case of education. Some children have to walk at least 5 kilometres to

Offei Hanson with his wives, children and local schoolchildren. Some of these children have to walk five kilometres to school.

The Hanson and Belle families sell their produce and buy household goods at this market in Anum-Apapam. The green bananas on sale here are plantains, which are delicious fried.

attend primary school, and the nearest secondary school is 60 kilometres away in Koforidua.

The people of Asikasu-Odumase are concerned about anything that affects the profitability of their farming, particularly weed infestation. One weed is causing a lot of trouble here. It is called acheampong stringa. The farmers have contacted their local agricultural office to see if they can advise on how to get rid of this pest. The people also want the road network, linking them to local towns, improved. This would assist in the sale of their produce.

The wealth associated with cocoa production has allowed these two farming families to put time and money into ensuring a good quality of life, now and in the future.

'There are no organizations or charities working here. We've constructed our own latrines and also created sources for getting water into our daily lives.'
– **Offei Hanson, cocoa farmer, Asikasu-Odumase, Eastern Region**

Sapeliga

This is a map of the chiefdom of Sapeliga in Ghana's Upper East Region.

Sapeliga is a remote chiefdom over thirteen hours' drive from Accra. Here, Ghana's savannah begins to merge with the Sahel. Six thousand people live in this area of widespread poverty where life is hard. People greet each other by saying, *'Tuma, tuma'* ('Work, work'). Compared to prosperous Asikasu-Odumase, development has passed Sapeliga by.

Ninety per cent of people in Sapeliga are farmers, mainly with small plots of land. There are a few wealthy people, called *arzak-daan*, who have modern dwellings, large farms, several cattle, bullocks and ploughs. However, 70 per cent are *sorsor-daan*

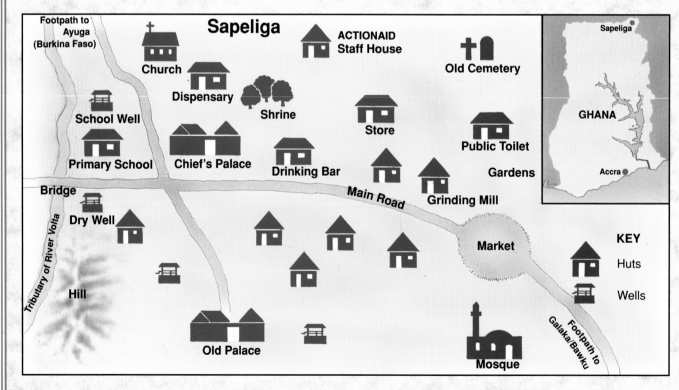

Women in the countryside have many responsibilities. As well as working in the fields and collecting water and fuelwood, they look after the children and cook for their families.

or *nong-daan*, poor farmers. While the *sorsor-daan* can provide just enough for themselves throughout the year, the *nong-daan* often cannot afford to buy seed for planting.

The staple crop in Sapeliga is millet. It is used to make people's main food, a millet porridge called *tuo zaafi* (TZ). Life here is organized around the cycle of millet planting and harvesting. There are two seasons. The hungry season is in July, when the fields are green with crops but people's granaries are empty. This is followed by the harvest in December, when the earth is parched brown but the millet crop has ripened. During times of hardship, many men migrate south to seek paid work on cocoa farms like the one owned by Offei Hanson in Asikasu-Odumase.

Poverty is so acute in Sapeliga that some people cannot afford to carry out their social obligations, such as funerals and marriages. To prevent people falling into debt, the customary length of a funeral was reduced from twelve to seven days, and the dowry amount was halved.

'Traditions must bow to conditions.'
– Chief Baba Ayagiba, Sapeliga

A development charity employee talks with a community to discover how they would like to improve their quality of life.

The development charity ACTIONAID decided to start development work in Sapeliga because of the area's high rate of poverty. Instead of telling the local community what the charity could do for them, the charity's development workers asked the people of Sapeliga to complete an exercise called participatory rural appraisal (PRA). This asks people to describe their local conditions and then to identify what help they want. The people of Sapeliga demonstrated to the development workers how the rains affected the cropping season, which in turn influenced when certain diseases were common.

Food security, education, safe drinking water and health care were identified as priorities. Food security means having enough food, or enough money to buy food, throughout the year. The main problems in ensuring food security in Sapeliga were low yields, poor storage facilities and lack of money.

ACTIONAID could have given people food when they ran out during the hungry season. This would have helped for one year, but people would still have faced the same problem in the future. Instead, a seed credit scheme was started. Over 1,700 farmers were each lent six bowls of sorghum or millet seed, or three bowls of groundnut seed, at the start of the planting season. After people had harvested their crops, they banked some of their harvest, plus an extra bowl of sorghum or millet, or half a bowl of groundnuts, as interest on the seed they had borrowed. This is a lower rate of interest than local traders charge. The banked seeds were then carefully stored in a metal container, guaranteeing that the

'I suggest after seed credit we need credit for bullocks and ploughs, and also cash credit, so we can start other businesses!' **– Atubilla Akpekire, Sapeliga**

farmers would have seeds for the next season. The scheme was a success, and the farmers would like it expanded.

These seasonal calendars, produced by the people of Sapeliga, show how rainfall affects harvesting and how times of ill health coincide with times of hunger.

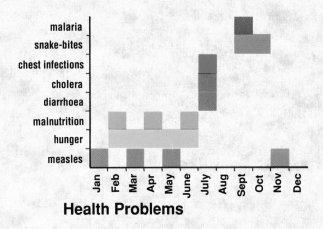

Health Problems

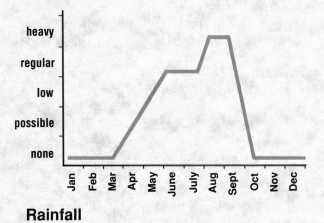

Rainfall

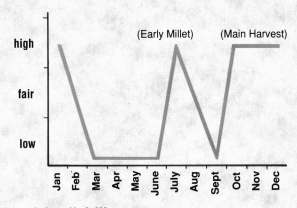

Food Availability

'I don't go to school because of my father's two cows, which I must look after.'
– Asake Ayebo, aged twelve, Sapeliga

In this primary school in Sapeliga the floor doubles as a blackboard.

Only 17 per cent of Sapeliga's children are enrolled in schools. Poverty, few teaching resources and the pressures of farm work on children's time reduce educational opportunities. When charity workers arrived, many of the classrooms did not have roofs, so lessons had to be stopped when it rained or was too hot.

Together, the development charity and local community refurbished five classrooms at three primary schools. New houses were built for teachers to encourage them to live in this remote area. The charity provided craftspeople and materials that were

'I've a hundred children in Class One with five books. How can this satisfy anyone's demand to learn?' – David Akoiis, teacher, Sapeliga

not available locally, such as cement, roofing sheets, paint and glass. The local community contributed unskilled labour, sand, stones, and accommodation and food for the craftspeople.

Thirty-four adult education classes were also set up. Reading materials, lamps and radios were provided. The radios were used to pick up literacy lessons broadcast from Bolgatanga, the district capital.

Water is a precious commodity in Sapeliga. In 1992 a survey found that nine out of eighteen bore holes were broken. They had fallen into disrepair because of a lack of money for parts, and the local community could not afford the rent on the wells. Many hand-dug wells dry up in the dry season, so women were having to walk long distances to collect water. The charity and local community repaired some wells and established well-management committees so that people could keep them working.

Sapeliga's health centre was rundown, and the nearest hospital was 40 kilometres away at Bawku. There was no immunization programme and few services for pregnant women. Now the community and charity have improved the health centre. It also has an immunization programme.

'The clinic helps children and adults, and the number of deaths has reduced. We don't need to transport sick people in donkey carts over long distances to get them treated.'
– Abariche Agura, Sapeliga

Eighteen traditional birth attendants (TBAs) – women who are untrained midwives – have been educated in the importance of health, hygiene and nutrition during pregnancy. By June 1992 over 250 pregnant women were receiving advice from the TBAs.

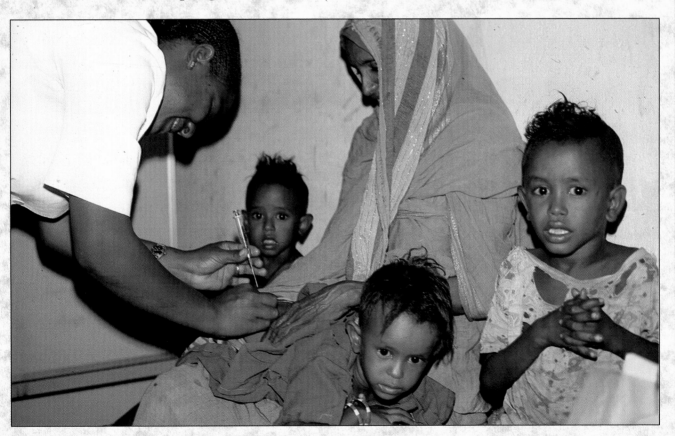

This child is bravely having his immunization injections. Immunization protects children from common diseases like polio and tetanus. These diseases can cause a high number of deaths in young children.

The future of Ghana

Ghana has achieved an improved standard of living for many of its people. This has been done through the co-operation of individuals, communities, businesses, the government, and international charities and organizations. Ghana's undoubted successes make it a good example of development.

Ghana has also recently discovered new opportunities for development, such as the tourist industry. Its income from tourism increased from $81 million in 1990 to $138 million in 1992.

One of Ghana's notable successes has been in the reduction of its infant mortality rate, which fell from 111 deaths per 1,000 births in 1970 to 93 deaths per 1,000 births in 1991. Infant mortality rate is a very sensitive measure of development. It highlights many important aspects of people's lives, such as child nutrition, the nutritional status of a pregnant woman, the awareness of health education messages and the provision of medical services during birth.

Another very positive sign for Ghana's future is its peaceful transition to democracy. Elections were held in November 1992, allowing the Ghanaian people to choose who they wanted to lead them. Jerry Rawlings was elected president of Ghana with 60 per cent of the vote. These democratic elections gave Ghana a better reputation internationally, which is vital if it is to continue to receive international support for its development work.

The Structural Adjustment Programme brought in by Rawlings has placed the Ghanaian economy

These tourists provide a new source of wealth for Ghana. Many link their holiday in the sun with a visit to see Ghana's wildlife.

The 1992 elections ran smoothly and were a very positive sign for Ghana's future. This man's thumb is dyed with a strong ink. Each voter had this dye applied so officials could make sure that no one voted twice.

on a more stable footing. Not everyone benefited from these changes. In response to criticism of the Structural Adjustment Programme, the government set up the Programme of Action to Mitigate the Social Costs of Adjustment (PAMSCAD). This organization will run programmes designed to help the poorest in Ghanaian society. PAMSCAD has already identified northern Ghana as one area where people's situation has worsened because of structural adjustment.

From the bustling cities to remote rural areas, Ghanaians have worked hard to improve their lives. In particular, they have a strong desire for their children to be educated and to have a better future. The case studies have demonstrated that, when they are given the opportunity, people can achieve positive changes in their lives.

The development aim for most Ghanaians is perhaps best captured in a saying from Sapeliga. When people think of the future, they often say, *'Ke te pam te meng,'* which means, 'Become independent and self-sufficient in your own affairs.'

'We'll provide the action if you provide the aid!'
– Chief Baba Aygiba, Sapeliga

45

Glossary

Bauxite   An ore that is used to make aluminium.

Bore hole   A deep, narrow hole made in the earth to find water.

Cedi   The currency used in Ghana.

Gross National Product (GNP) per capita   The total wealth a country produces, within its borders and from trade, divided by the number of people in that country.

Hydroelectric power   Electricity produced by flowing water, which drives a generator.

Import substitution   The production of goods that used to be imported into a country.

Infant mortality rate   The number of children who die before their fifth birthday.

Life expectancy   The average age to which someone can expect to live.

Official development assistance   Grants and loans given to help poor countries pay for development work.

Petty trader   Someone who makes a living selling small amounts of fruit, vegetables or household goods.

Population density   The number of people who live in a country, divided by the country's land area. This is shown as the number of people per square kilometre.

Privatized   Sold by a government to private investors.

Savannah   Large plains of grassland.

Slum   An area of very poor quality housing, usually with few services such as running water and electricity.

Structural Adjustment Policies (SAPs)   A series of changes made to improve the running of a country's economy.

Further information

ACTIONAID, Hamlyn House, Archway, London N19 5PG, provides information on Ghana and other developing countries.

The Commonwealth Institute, Kensington High Street, London W8 6NQ, has a permanent display on Ghana and provides free information leaflets on Ghana and other Commonwealth countries.

The Development Education Association, 3rd Floor, Cowper Street, London EC2A 4AP, can provide the address of a resource centre near you that has information on Ghana and other developing countries.

Addokorpe: Life in a Ghanaian Village (Worldvision/Worldaware) is a photo pack exploring village life, available from Worldaware, 1 Catton Street, London WC1R 4AB.

Cheraponi: Ghanaian Village Life (ACTIONAID) is a photo pack exploring village life in northern Ghana, available from ACTIONAID, 3 Church Street, Frome, Somerset BA11 1PW.

State of the World's Children is an annual report with information about developing countries, available from UNICEF, 55-56 Lincoln's Inn Fields, London WC2A 3NB.

Books to read

Chocolate Unwrapped: The Politics of Pleasure by Cat Cox (Women's Environmental Network, 1993) explores the production, marketing and consumption of cocoa and chocolate.

Comfort Herself by Geraldine Kaye (Deutsch, 1984). The story of a girl whose father is Ghanaian and mother is English and her experience of Ghanaian and English life.

Water (Birmingham Development Education Centre, 1990), a photo pack exploring the importance of water, available from DEC, Selly Oak Colleges, Bristol Road, Selly Oak, Birmingham B29 6LE.

Index

Numbers in **bold** refer to illustrations.